The Printable Staff Paper Page, by David Anthony Borrell II

http://fr

3345 5432 1123 322
3345 5432 1123 211

The Joy of First-Year Piano

A method and repertory for the beginning pianist

by Denes Agay

THE JOY OF FIRST-YEAR PIANO is a book for beginners of all ages. Its purpose is to provide a slowly and meticulously graded repertory of appealing pieces through which the beginning pianist can acquire the fundamentals of note-reading and playing in an effortless and pleasurable manner. The sequence of these little pieces is planned to introduce new concepts step-by-step, to give opportunity for frequent repetition of things already learned, and to allow all information to be absorbed before progressing further.

The course is a flexible one, leaving the teacher several options, depending on the age and ability of the student. It is recommended that the average young beginner, between the ages of approximately six and nine, be given all introductory material, including rote pieces and the playing by finger numbers (pages 4 to 10). On the same pages, older beginners can acquire the necessary basic information about the keyboard, the staff, note-values, etc., in an accelerated manner and may actually begin by reading and playing the first pieces on page 11.

This volume uses middle-C as the focus of orientation in teaching note-reading, because of its indisputable visual logic. At the same time, however, the student is led from the very beginning to play certain pieces in octave transpositions, with the right hand placed an octave higher, and the left an octave lower. Thus he is given an opportunity from the outset to play in various hand positions, thereby gaining flexibility and strain-free use of the arm, wrist, and hand muscles.

A famous novelist, Maxim Gorky, was once asked by a young writer how to write for children. Gorky's answer was this: "You write for children the same way you write for grownups, *only better*." This had been the guiding thought in the preparation of this volume. Writing for the beginner pianist requires as much, and possibly even more imagination, inventiveness and craftsmanship than composing for the expert. With the very limited means, often only a few notes at his disposal, the composer of beginners' pieces has to create music which not only introduces specific teaching matters, but also is simple, well-formed and attractive. These pieces must have the quality to engage and stimulate the student's interest, guide him toward developing a sound musical taste, motivate further study, and, in general, foster the love of music.

We hope that THE JOY OF FIRST-YEAR PIANO fulfills these goals.

All pieces, unless otherwise identified, are by Denes Agay.

Order No. YK 21053
US International Standard Book Number: 0.8256.8013.1
UK International Standard Book Number: 0.7119.0123.6

Exclusive Distributors:
Music Sales Corporation
257 Park Avenue South, New York, NY 10010 USA
Music Sales Limited
8/9 Frith Street, London W1V 5TZ England
Music Sales Pty. Limited
120 Rothschild Street, Rosebery, Sydney NSW 2018 Australia

Printed in the United States of America by
Vicks Lithograph and Printing Corporation

Contents

The Correct Position At The Piano

Sit facing the middle of the keyboard with both feet firmly on the floor in front of the pedals. (A foot-stool or box should be used if the feet of small children do not reach the floor.)

Allow the upper arm to hang loosely. Adjust the seat so that the fore-arm, wrist and hand are in line with the keyboard.

Do not lean back in the chair with your full weight. The entire body should be relaxed; the back straight, without stiffness, with just a hint of leaning forward ever so slightly.

The hands should be vaulted, with palms, down, and should assume a shape as if lightly upholding a small round object, like a ball.

The fingers should be gently curved, with the fleshy part of the finger tips (not the nails) touching the keys.

How To Practice

Before playing a piece, place your hands on the keyboard in the proper five-finger position, as indicated by the finger-number of the starting note in each hand. Maintain the hand position throughout the piece, unless a new finger-number indicates a shift of hand position.

Within a given hand position finger-numbers are given only sparingly. This is to stimulate the player to *read* every note instead of being guided merely by the fingering marks. At the teacher's discretion additional finger-numbers may be, of course, written in.

Wherever a note chart is given under the title of a piece, first play these notes calling out their letter-names. The letter-names may also be written under each note of the chart, especially under notes occuring for the first time. If necessary, new notes may also be looked up or located on the comprehensive note chart on page 10.

Never try to guess what the next note is; you should *know* it before striking the key.

Practice slowly at first, always at an even pace and in strict rhythm. As a preliminary exercise you may clap the rhythm of the melody before playing it. Most of the time you should also count aloud when practicing a piece.

Pieces in the first half of the book should also be practiced by singing the letter-names of the keys while playing the melody.

Always *listen* to what you are playing.

Pieces to be taught by rote (imitation)

- See footnotes on next page -

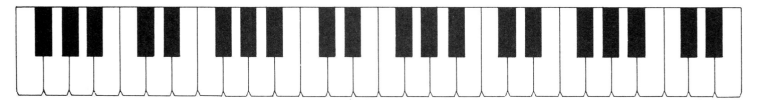

- This is the KEYBOARD of the piano.

- You sit at the piano facing the middle of the keyboard.

- The keyboard has white keys and black keys.

- The white keys are in a row. The black keys are arranged in groups of two's and three's. (Point out these groups of two and three black keys)*

- All keys, black and white, produce different tones.   Going to the right, or going "up" the keyboard, the tones become gradually higher.   Going to the left, or going "down" the keyboard, the tones become gradually lower.   High notes are to the right, low notes to the left. **

- Look at the drawing of the two hands. For the purpose of playing the piano our fingers are numbered.   The thumb is the first finger on each hand.

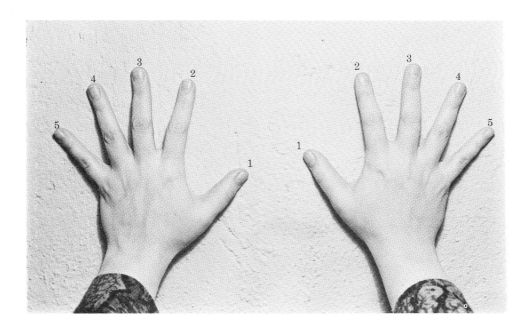

Learn the number of each finger this way: hold your hands in front of you and move each finger as its number is called out by your teacher. At first practice this separately with each hand, then with the two hands together. ***

---

* Pieces numbered 1 and 2 (on preceding page) may be taught here by imitation.

** Pieces numbered 3, 4 and 5 may be taught here.

*** Piece No. 6 can be given here.   Fingering is optional; right hand: 4-3-2, 3-2-1, or 5-4-3; left hand: 2-3 or 1-2.

- Place your hands on the keyboard as shown in the picture.   Fingers should be curved touching the keys lightly.

hands in C position

With your hands in this position, using all five fingers one by one, as shown by the finger-numbers, play these melodies and sing out the number of each finger. (Press the keys down gently but firmly; finger tips should maintain their firm, curved position.)

Left hand   Right hand

```
         1                    1 —              5 — 5
           2                2               4          4
a.)          3          3                 3            3
              4       4                 2              2
               5 — 5                  1                 1 —
```

Left hand   Right hand

```
       1          1 — 1              5          5 — 5
                      2                                  4
b.)    3      3         3            3      3         3
                        4                                 2
        5 — 5        5 —           1 — 1              1 —
```

a.)

b.)

-Here is another melody you can play by the finger-numbers. Maintain the same hand
position as shown on the opposite page. First sing out the finger-numbers while playing, then sing the words.

```
                                                5
                                        4   top  4
c.)  Right hand                       3   the      and  3
                          2   2   2  —  To            down  2
          1   1   1  —  Here we  go,                    we   1  —
          Here  we  go,                                      go.
                                                1
                                        2   top  2
d,)  Left hand                        3   the      and  3
                          4   4   4  —  To            down  4
          5   5   5  —  Here we  go,                    we   5  —
          Here  we  go,                                      go.
```

- Now try to to play "Here We Go" in another position on the keyboard.
Place your fingers on the keys as indicated by the finger-numbers.
(Notice that the third finger is placed on a black key.)

- Sing again "Here We Go" and this time clap your hands as you sing:

```
Sing: Here we go,  | Here we go,  | To  the  top  and | down we go.  ‖
Clap hands:  *  *  *  *  |  *  *  *  *  |  *  *  *  *  |  *  *  *  *  ‖
```

Did you notice that every time you sang the word "go" you clapped your hands twice,
while singing the other words you clapped only once? This means that the note sung
to the word "go" is held twice as long as the notes sung to the other words; it receives
two counts while the other words receive one count.

> This is a one-count note ♩ called QUARTER-NOTE
>
> This is a two-count note ♩ called HALF-NOTE
>
> This is a four-count note ○ called WHOLE-NOTE

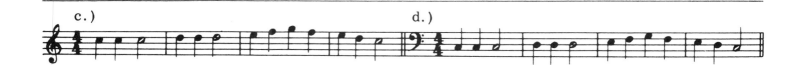

-Knowing the finger numbers and also how long to hold the notes, you will be able to play these melodies. (Do you recognize them?) Keep the same hand position as pictured on page 6.

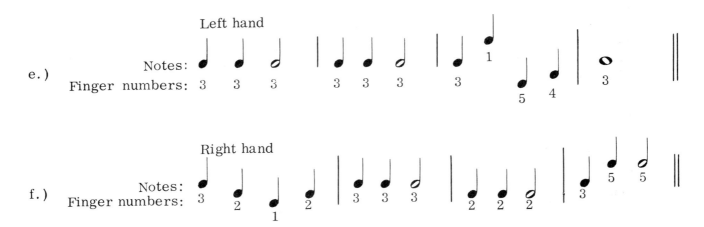

e.) Left hand
Notes:
Finger numbers: 3 3 3   3 3 3   3   5 4   1   3

f.) Right hand
Notes:
Finger numbers: 3 2 1 2   3 3 3   2 2 2   3   5 5

-Look again carefully at the notes of the melodies you have just played ("Jingle Bells" and "Mary Had a Little Lamb"). You can see that the notes always follow the rise and fall of the melody. When the melody goes up, the notes go up too; when the melody goes down, so do the notes. In order to see exactly how high or low a note should be placed, we need some guide lines. These guide lines are called the STAFF.

This the STAFF 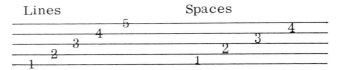 It has five lines and, between the lines, four spaces.

The lines and spaces are numbered from the bottom up:

Lines   Spaces
5
4   4
3   3
2   2
1   1

The notes are placed both on the lines and in the spaces:

-In piano music we use two staffs, connected by a brace: This staff, headed by the TREBLE CLEF, is for higher notes, usually played by the right hand.

This staff, headed by the BASS CLEF, is for lower notes, usually played by the left hand.

e.)   f.)

- To make notes easier to follow
the staff is divided by BAR LINES
into MEASURES:

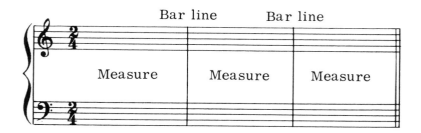

- The two numbers placed after the clefs are called the TIME SIGNATURE.
This is what the two numbers mean:

2 The upper number shows how many counts are in a measure (two)
4 The lower number shows what kind of note receives one count (quarter note)

- What do these time singnatures mean ?   **3/4**   **4/4**

Counting Exercises

- Clap your hands for every note, counting aloud the proper number of beats in each
measure. (Remember, some notes are held for one count and others for two counts.)

Count: one   two,   one-two   (etc.)

Count: one-two - three, one-two-three, (etc.)

Count:

-Play again "Jingle Bells" and "Mary Had a Little Lamb" (on top of page 8).
This time do not sing the words but count "one-two-three-four" in each measure.

The Letter-Names of the Keys

-The white keys of the keyboard are named after the first seven letters of the alpha-
bet: A - B - C - D - E - F - G.

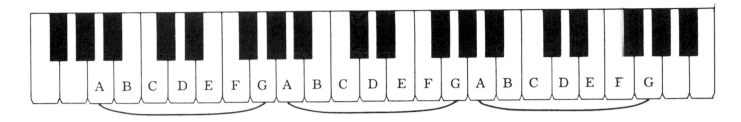

- C's are to the left of the two black keys.   Find all C's on your piano.   Find the MIDDLE C.

-Play the Middle C. What is the letter-name of the next key to the left?   And the
 next key to the right?

-Play all C-D-E's (touching the two black keys).

-Find all A's (to the left of the third black key).

-Play all A-B-C's.

-Play A-B-C-D-E.

-Find all F-G's (touching the first of the three black keys).

Note Chart

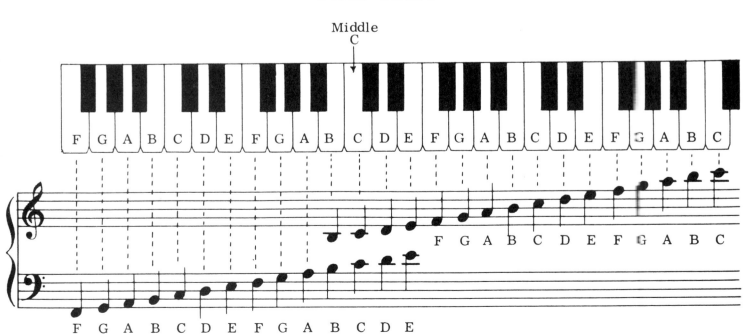

Three - Note Jig

Play Tune

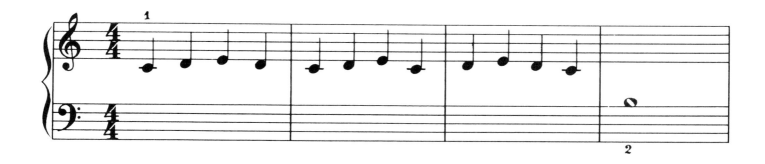

Optional duet part
for "Play Tune"

♩. DOTTED HALF-NOTE
(Three counts)

First Serenade

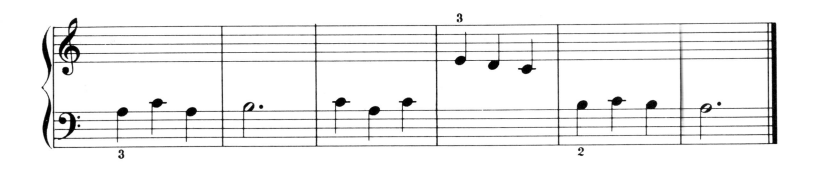

Optional
duet part

Mysterious Procession

(right hand repeats the same note throughout)

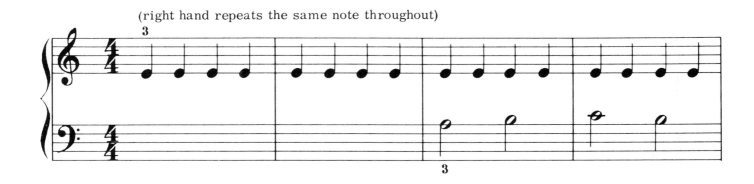

Play "Mysterious Procession" also this way: place the right hand an OCTAVE (eight keys) higher and the left hand an octave lower.

Bluebird

Play Tune, U.S.A.

Blue-bird, blue-bird, on my shoul-der, Blue-bird, blue-bird, on my shoul-der,

Blue-bird, blue-bird on my shoul-der, John-ny I am ti-red.

Optional duet part

f (*forte*) = loud
p (*piano*) = soft

Pleading Child

Hopscotch

The WHOLE-REST 𝄻 indicates silence in one whole measure of any kind.

Little Song

Optional duet part for "Little Song"

The HALF-REST ▬ indicates silence for two counts; it has the same time value as the half-note.

▬ = 𝅗𝅥 = two counts

Good King Wenceslas

Ancient Carol

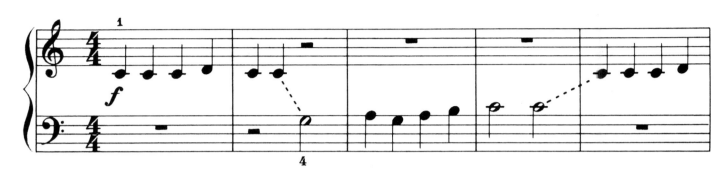

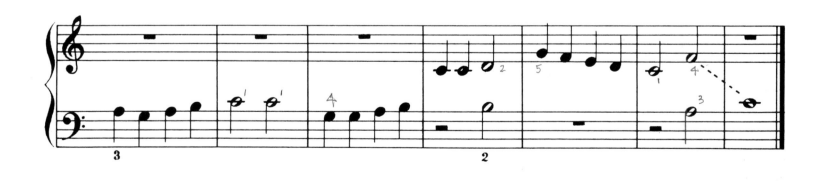

Optional
duet part

The SHARP sign ♯ raises the note to the next higher note; you play the nearest key to the right, black or white.

On the Merry-Go-Round

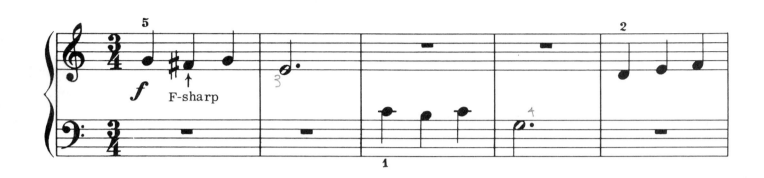

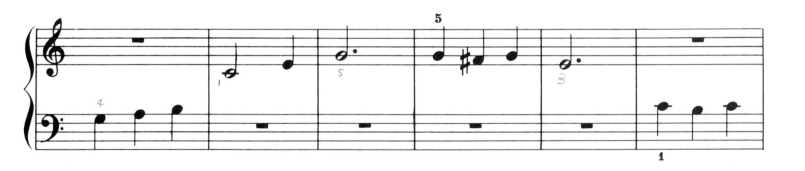

Optional
duet part

18

mf (*mezzo-forte*) = medium loud

Old-World Melody

Optional duet part

The QUARTER-REST 𝄽 indicates silence for one count; it equals the time value of a quarter-note.
𝄽 = ♩ = one count

Spring Morning

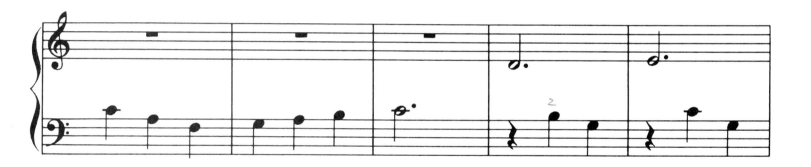

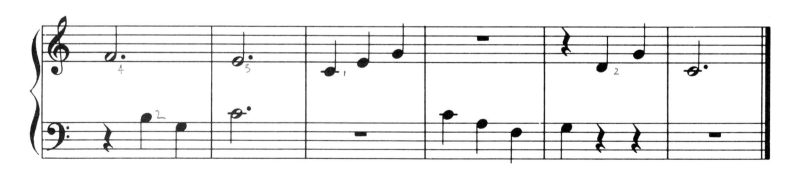

Optional duet part

A melody can start on any beat of the measure.   This one starts on the fourth count.

Cathedral Bells

English Folk Song

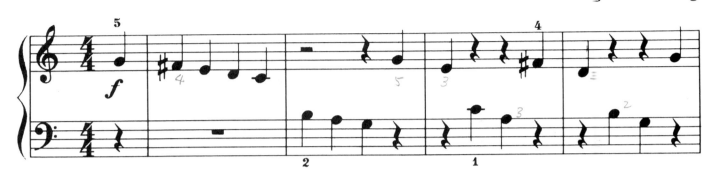

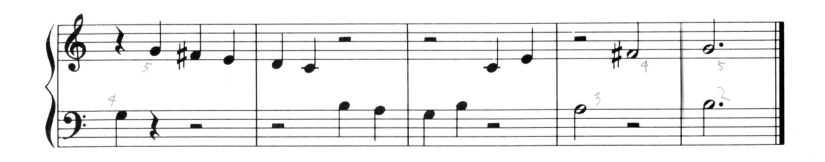

Optional
duet part

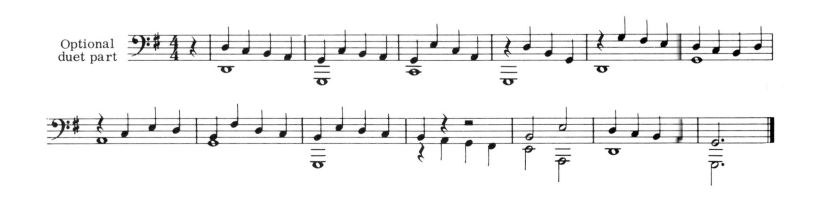

The FLAT sign ♭ lowers a note; you play the nearest key to the left, black or white.

Over Hill and Dale

B-flat

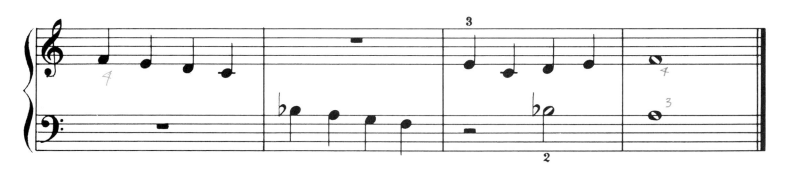

Greeting from Jamaica

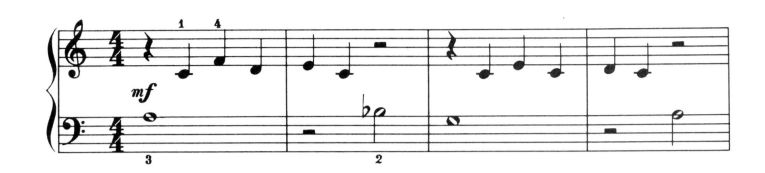

Hebrew Melody

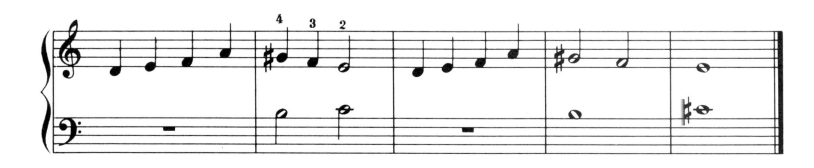

The SLUR, a curved line over two or more notes, is the sign of *legato*; these notes are to be played in a smooth, connected manner.

Romance

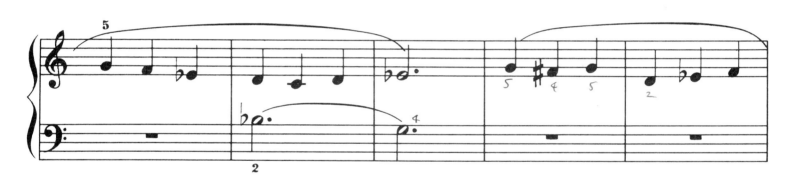

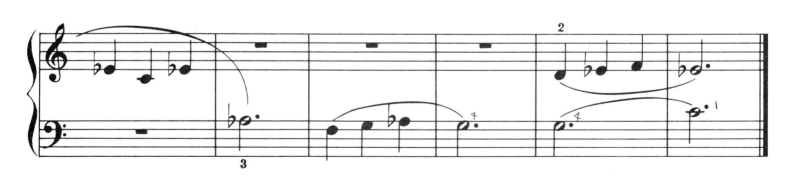

Optional duet part

Two EIGHTH-NOTES $\left(\text{♫}\right)$ equal the time value of one quarter-note $\left(\text{♩}\right)$

♩ = ♫ = one count

Skip To My Lou

Folk Tune, U.S.A.

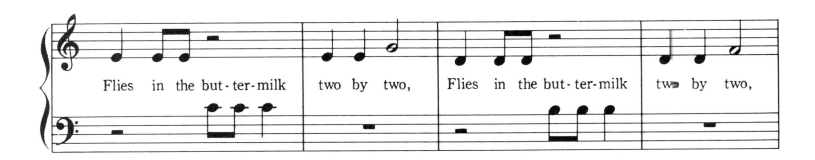

Optional duet part

Parade

The TIE is a curved line connecting two neighboring notes of the same sound (pitch).   You play only the first note and <u>hold the second note</u> for its full time value.

Dusk and Dawn

Rather slow

Repeat piece; this time play *mf* and raise all F's to F-sharp.

Little Prelude

Moderately

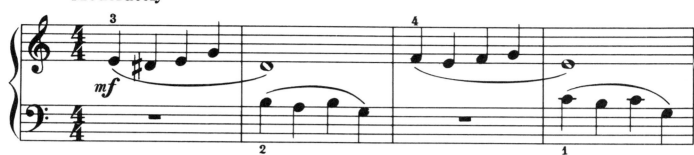

Review the meaning of the following words and signs:

1. *f* and *p*
2. LEGATO
3. 𝄽
4. The TIE
5. The SHARP sign (♯)

6. The SLUR
7. The FLAT sign (♭)
8. ▬
9. An OCTAVE
10. *mf* (*mezzo - forte*)

Playful Dialogue

German Children's Song

> =accent mark

Roundelay

Gaily

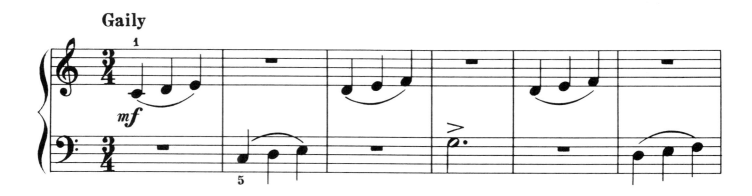

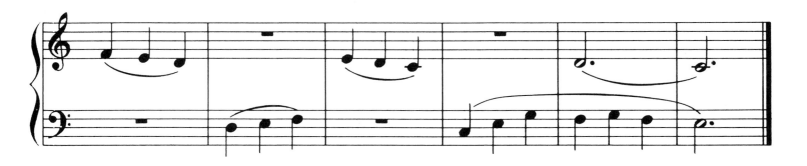

Lightly Row

German Song

Moderately

Play the piece again, this time placing your right hand an octave higher.

Sharps and flats alter not only the note in front of which they are placed, but also all other notes of the same letter-name <u>in that one measure.</u>

Melody

Antonio Diabelli

Play the piece again, this time placing your right hand an octave higher.

Ancient Chinese Song

Optional duet part

Blue Interlude

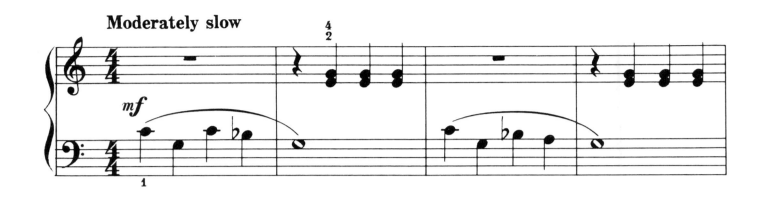

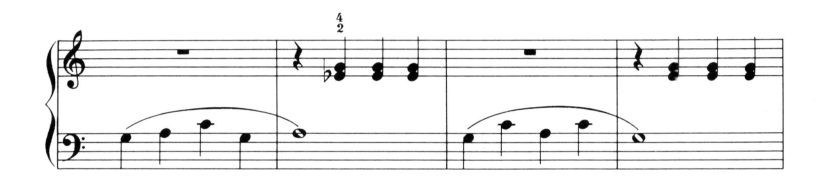

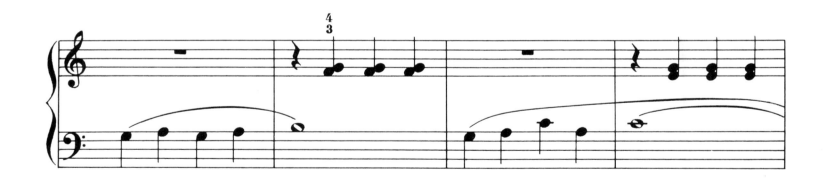

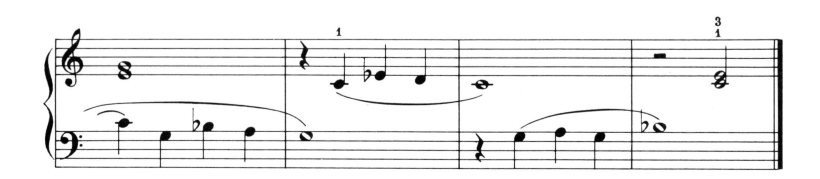

The Merry Cossacks

crescendo = gradually louder

decrescendo or diminuendo = gradually softer

Drifting Clouds

Gently moving

Sea Chantey

With energy

Way, hey! up she ris - es, Way, hey! up she ris - es,

Way, hey! up she ris - es ear - ly in the morn - ing.

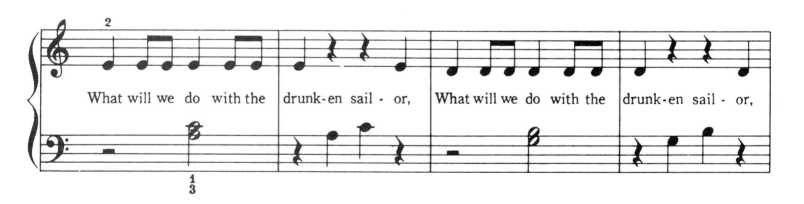

What will we do with the drunk-en sail - or, What will we do with the drunk-en sail - or,

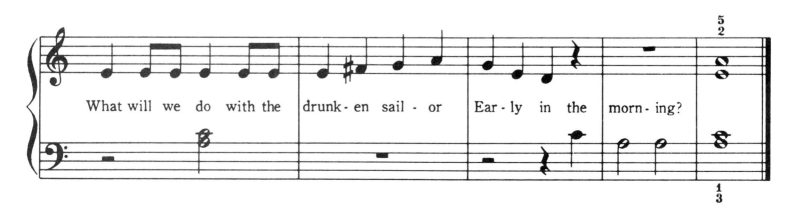

What will we do with the drunk-en sail - or Ear - ly in the morn - ing?

rit. (*ritardando*) = gradually slower

Eventide

A small dot at the note-head $\left(\dot{} \right)$ is the sign of *staccato:* you play that note in a short, detached manner. After striking the key, the finger returns instantly to its raised position.

Dancing Raindrops

The Railroad Corral

Gaily

Cowboy Song

We're— up in the morn-ing ere break of the day, The—

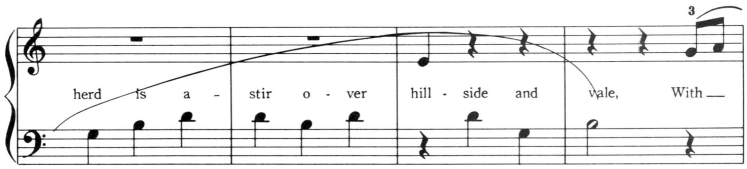

chuck wag-on's bus-y, the flap-jack's in play. The

herd is a - stir o - ver hill-side and vale, With—

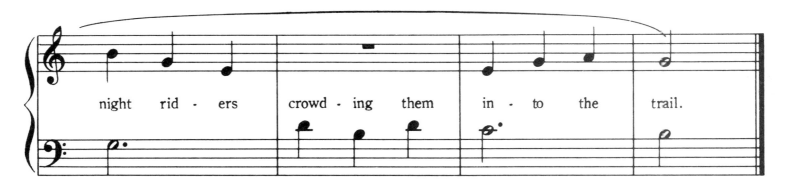

night rid-ers crowd-ing them in - to the trail.

Try to play this piece again as if it had a flat in front of each note. (You'll play on black keys with the exception of the C-flats.)

A small dash at the note-head $\left(\underset{\cdot}{\downarrow} \right)$ is the sign of *tenuto*. It means that you hold down the key for the note's full time value.

Cotillion Polka

Moderately lively

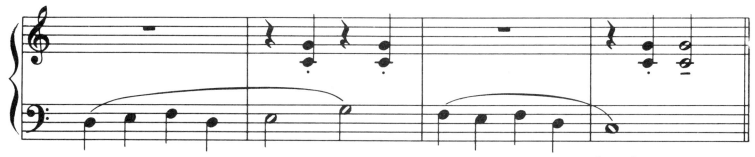

Repeat from beginning to *Fine*.
Fine (fee-neh) is an Italian term meaning End.

40

Sailors' Dance

Lively

Danish Folk Dance

left hand

Fine

Repeat from
beginning to *Fine*

This sign 8----- means that you play the notes under the dotted line an octave higher.
pp (*pianissimo*) = very soft

Monastery Echoes

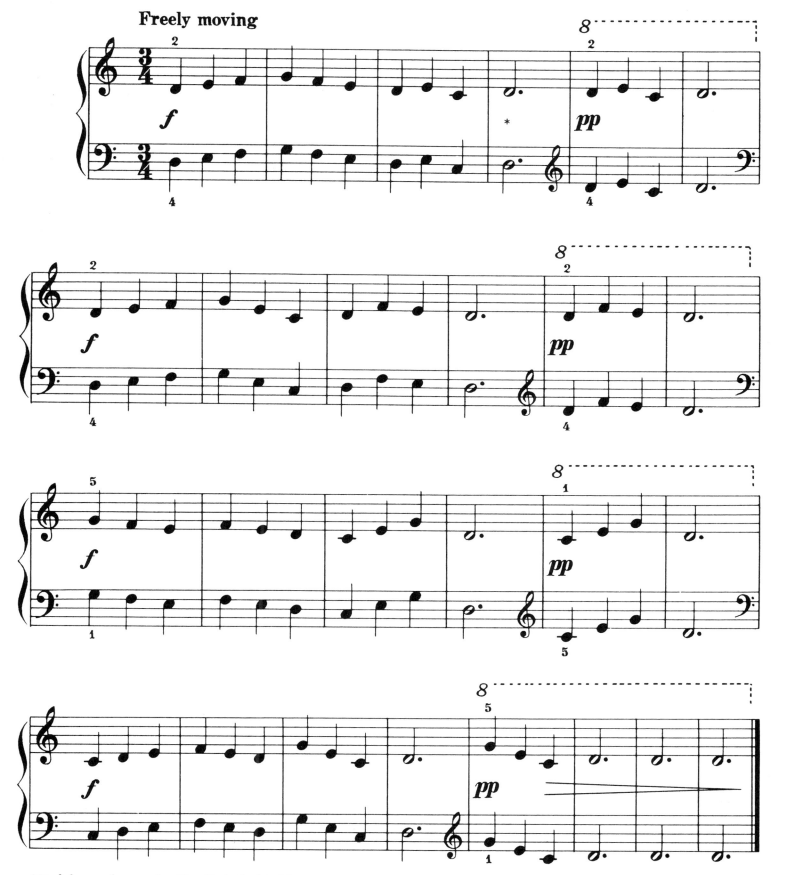

*Pedal may be used with all dotted half-notes.

Balkan Bagatelle

Lullaby for a French Doll

French Folk Song

C , as a time signature, is the same as 4/4

The Bagpipers

Lively

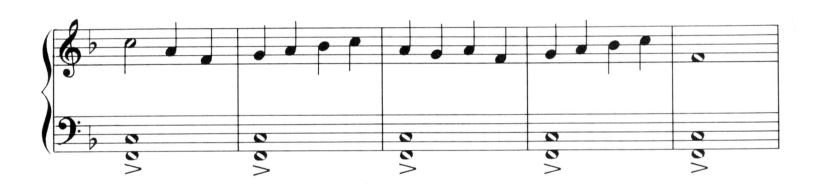

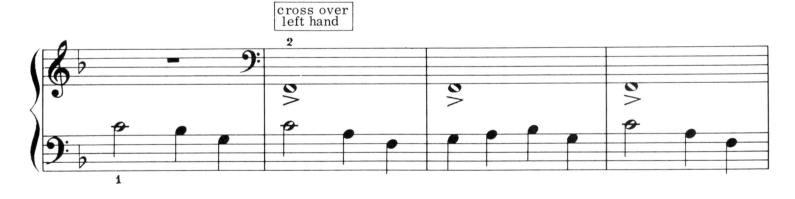

cross over
left hand

Fiddler's Holiday

Marian

Moderately

West-Indian Folk Tune

Key signature
(F major)

Frolic

Use the third finger only in both hands.

Gaily hopping

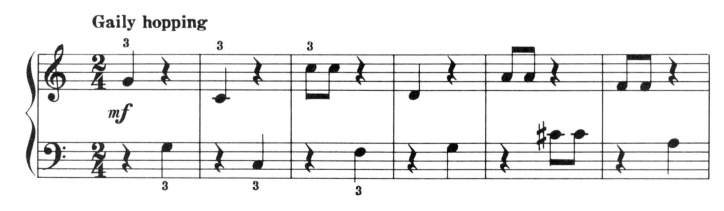

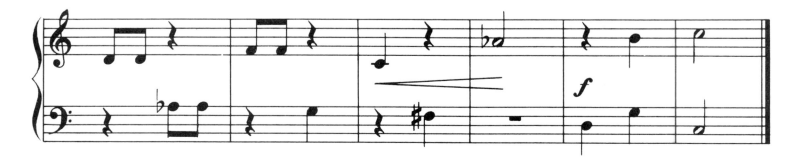

On a Green Meadow

Psalm Without Words

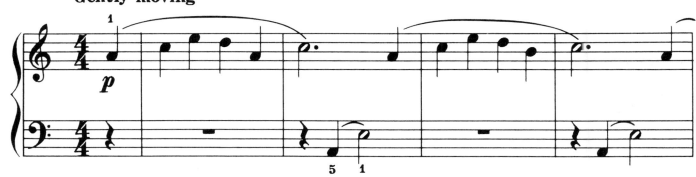

Gently moving

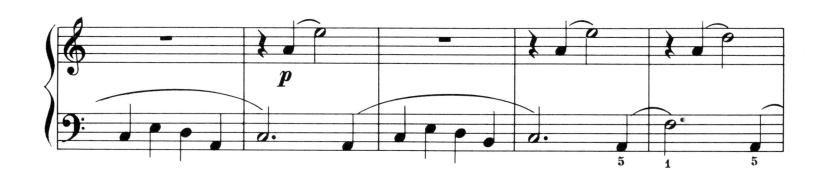

Shepherd's Hay

English Folk Dance

On a Country Lane

50

This sign ♮ is called a NATURAL; it cancels a sharp or a flat, you play the original white key.
The three signs, *sharp, flat* and *natural,* are also called ACCIDENTALS.

Summer Afternoon

Miniature Sonatina

At the Circus

Song of the Gondolier

Ballet Scene

Fanfare

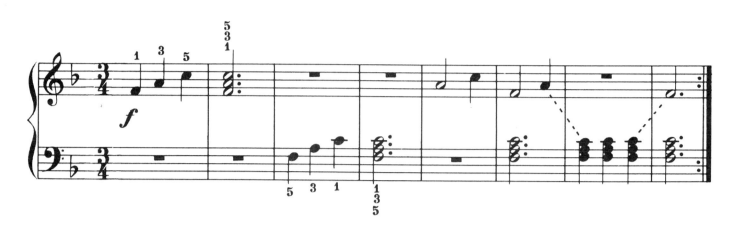

Love Somebody

Folk Tune, U.S.A.

Love some-bod - y, yes, I do, Love some-bod - y, yes, I do,

Love some-bod - y, yes, I do, And I won't tell who, who, who.

White Sails

Graceful, steady motion

Alexander March

Edited by Denes Agay

Ludwig van Beethoven

Brisk, walking tempo

Melody with Varied Accompaniments

Moody Twins

≻ = accented staccato

Wooden-Shoe Dance

The DOTTED QUARTER-NOTE

The Birch Tree

Russian Folk Song

Moderato

Repeat piece *f*

Canon*

Konrad M. Kunz

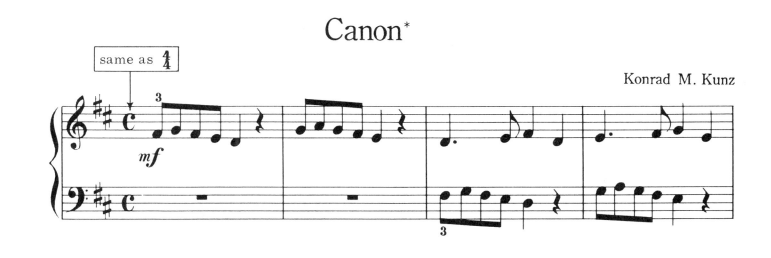

*Canon is a musical form in which a melody line is strictly imitated by another voice.

Theme and Variations

Moderato

Var. 1

Var. 2

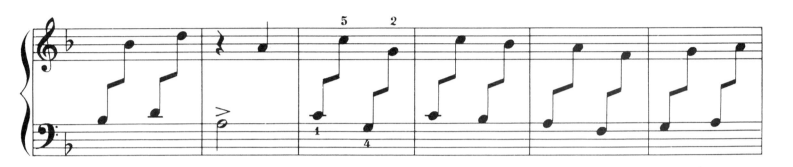

Game of Tag

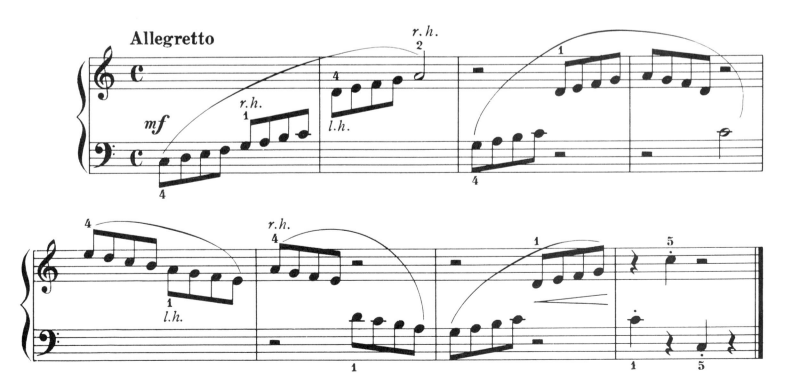

On the Playground

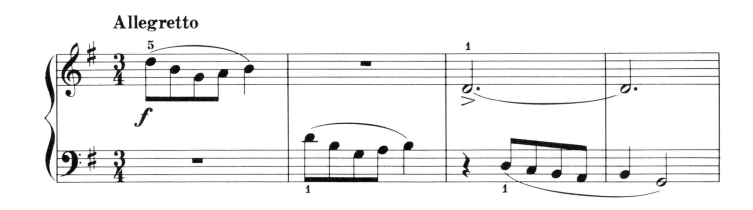

Allegretto

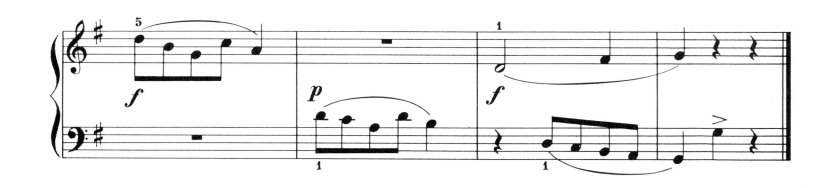

Play the five-note figures with a loose "down-up" motion of the wrist.

See-Saw Sonata

Courting Song

Partners in Melody

∧ = Very sharp accent

Squabble

Denes Agay

Idyl

Denes Agay

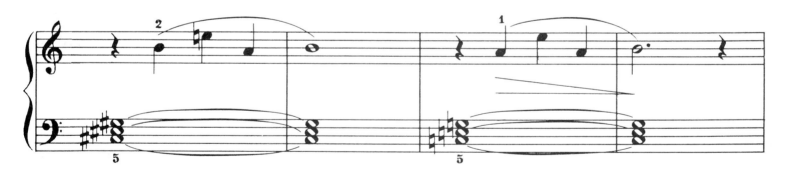

* In a singing manner.

Whistle - Stop Boogie

Steady beat (Moderate - to - brisk)

Gerald Martin

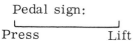

Moonlit Pagoda

Moderately ; gently moving

Denes Agay

Two SIXTEENTH-NOTES (♫) equal the time value of one eight-note ♪

Four sixteenth-notes (♬) equal the time value of one quarter-note ♩

♩ = ♫ = ♬ = ♬

I Danced with a Mosquito

Allegro

Russian Folk Song

English Dance

James Hook

Allegro

In $\frac{6}{8}$ time there are six counts in a measure; the eighth-note gets one count.
When playing in six-eight time, accents usually fall on the <u>first</u> and on the <u>fourth</u> beat.

Tap this rhythm:

Count: 1 2 3 4 5 6   1 2 3 4 5 6   1 2 3 4 5 6   1 2 3 4 5 6

Sally Go 'Round

English Play Tune

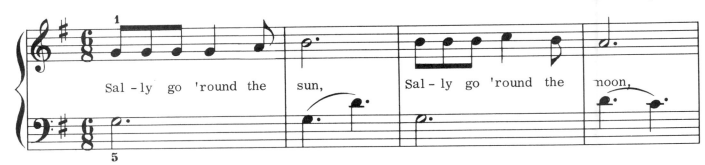

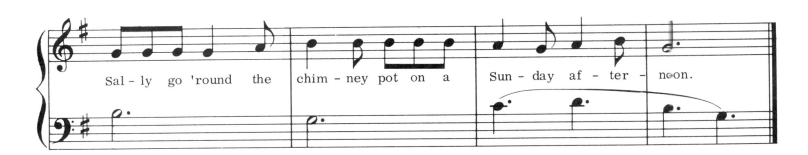

In the Swing

Andantino

The Brass Band

Village Fair

A. Nikolaiev

Repeat from this sign 𝄋

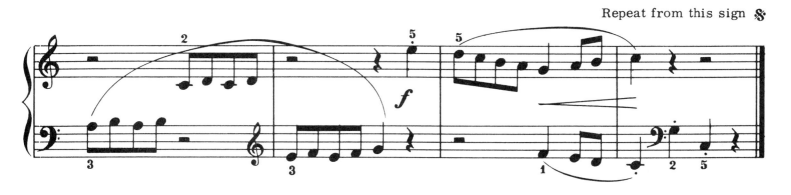

Three eighth-notes receiving one count are called a TRIPLET

♩ = ♫ = triplet figure = one count

Promenade

Ballad

Denes Agay

The DOTTED EIGHTH-NOTE

Mazurka

This piece is preparatory to the playing of scales. The passing of the thumb and the crossing of the third finger should be smooth, neither sluggish, nor hurried, without any unnecessary sudden motions of the wrist or the elbow.

Scale Capers

Using the same fingering, play this scale pattern in the keys of G, D, A, and E major.